COLORADO

Past and Present

Bridget Heos

rosen publishing's
rosen central®

New York

For my Papa and Nana, John and Gerry Gaughan, for all those trips to Estes Park

Published in 2011 by The Rosen Publishing Group, Inc.
29 East 21st Street, New York, NY 10010

Copyright © 2011 by The Rosen Publishing Group, Inc.

First Edition

Library of Congress Cataloging-in-Publication Data

Heos, Bridget.
Colorado : past and present / Bridget Heos.— 1st ed.
    p. cm. — (The United States: past and present)
Includes bibliographical references and index.
ISBN 978-1-4358-9477-8 (library binding)
ISBN 978-1-4358-9530-0 (pbk.)
ISBN 978-1-4358-9564-5 (6-pack)
 1. Colorado—Juvenile literature. I. Title.
F776.3.H46 2011
978.8—dc22

                                                              2010000419

Manufactured in Malaysia

CPSIA Compliance Information: Batch #S10YA: For further information, contact Rosen Publishing, New York, New York, at 1-800-237-9932.

On the cover: Top left: Colorado gold miners in 1880. Top right: Denver, the capital of Colorado and its largest city. Bottom: The Garden of the Gods.

Contents

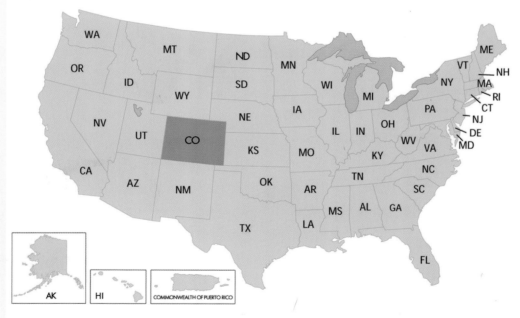

Colorado is bordered by Utah, Wyoming, Nebraska, Kansas, Oklahoma, New Mexico, and Arizona. The top five largest cities in Colorado are Denver, Colorado Springs, Aurora, Lakewood, and Fort Collins.

Introduction

Visitors to Rocky Mountain National Park in Colorado can hike along the Continental Divide National Scenic Trail. Along the way, they might see moose or elk in the woods. Then, as they climb higher than 12,000 feet (3,658 meters) above sea level, the fir trees give way to tundra. Here, long winters, heavy snow, and strong winds cause plants to "hug" the ground. They grow no higher than a foot (.3 m).

Finally, at 12,324 feet (3,756 m), hikers will reach the crest of the Rocky Mountains: the Continental Divide. To the east, all rivers eventually flow into the Gulf of Mexico. To the west, rivers empty into the Pacific Ocean. North and south, the Great Divide stretches from Alaska to South America. It is known as America's backbone.

Colorado has more than a thousand mountain peaks that stand taller than 10,000 feet (3,048 m). Mountain rain and melting snow create the headwaters of seven major rivers, which rush downhill in cascades of white water. The state is known for its snow-blanketed ski slopes and sunny summer days.

Unique natural features have always been a driving force in Colorado. Thousands of years ago, Native American tribes traveled to hot springs for their healing powers. In the 1800s, European Americans flocked to the state in pursuit of fur and gold. Even after mining declined, cities grew. Universities, hospitals, businesses, military bases, and the tourism industry became major employers. The beauty of the state drew visitors and new residents.

Chapter 1

THE GEOGRAPHY OF COLORADO

With the Rocky Mountains running through it, Colorado has a higher elevation than any other state. On average, it is 6,800 feet (2,073 m) above sea level. The highest point, Mount Elbert, is 14,431 feet (4,399 m). The lowest elevation is 3,315 feet (1,010 m) and lies in the southeastern part of the state in the Arkansas Valley. Even in the seemingly flat area from the Kansas border to Denver, the land is in fact sloping upward.

Greater Denver is a sprawling city that straddles the plains and foothills. Outside of Denver, the foothills give way to mountains. This is known as the Front Range of the Rocky Mountains.

The Continental Divide follows the crest of the Rocky Mountains from Alaska through Colorado and south to New Mexico. The climate varies on either side of the divide. Pacific Ocean storms travel to the western mountains, where they often become snowstorms. In the eastern mountains and plains, polar air from the north mingles with moist air from the south, creating blizzards. The Eisenhower Tunnel burrows underneath the Continental Divide. Because of the weather difference, drivers can enter the tunnel under clear skies and exit into a blizzard.

Most of the land in Colorado along the Continental Divide is part of the National Forest System. It contains miles of hiking trails and ski slopes—from Rocky Mountain National Park in the north to the San Juan Mountains in the south.

West of this area is the Colorado Plateau. Here, the landscape is diverse. The Grand Valley is known for its rich farmland, warm summers, and unique landforms, including mesas, canyons, and natural arches.

The climate varies widely in Colorado. Elevation is a huge factor. Pikes Peak (elevation 14,110 feet [4,301 m]) and Las Animas (elevation about 3,895 feet [1,187 m]) are 90 miles (145 kilometers) apart, but the difference between their mean temperatures is 35 degrees, which is approxi-

Mount Elbert is the highest point in Colorado. It is the second highest mountain peak in the continental United States after Mount Whitney.

mately the difference between Florida's and Iceland's mean temperatures. Snowfall also depends on elevation. In Cubres in the southern mountains, 300 inches (762 centimeters) of snow fall yearly, whereas 30 miles (48 km) away in Manassa, in the San Luis Valley, just 25 inches (64 cm) fall. In general, the eastern plains and western plateau have hot summers and milder winters, whereas the mountains are cooler year-round.

The Colorado National Monument is located in the Western Plateau region of Colorado. The area is known for its unique landforms, including mesas, canyons, and natural arches.

Despite heavy snowfalls, Colorado is known for its nice climate. The humidity is low, making warm days comfortable. The thin atmosphere lets in the sun, making cold days warmer. Colorado does have some severe weather, though. East of the Continental Divide, blizzards, thunderstorms, drought, and hail sometimes strike. In the mountains, heavy snowfall can cause avalanches. Rainstorms and snowmelts can cause terrible floods.

Rivers, Plants, and Animals

Snowmelt feeds several major rivers in Colorado, all of which originate in the state. West of the Continental Divide, the Colorado River begins its journey toward the Grand Canyon and, finally, the Pacific Ocean. East of the divide, the South Platte, Arkansas, and Rio Grande all eventually flow into the Gulf of Mexico.

The flooding of these rivers can be devastating. From 1864 to 1933, the South Platte River and its tributaries, including Clear Creek, Bear Creek, Plum Creek, and Cherry Creek, flooded low-lying areas of Denver about every ten years. By 1965, Denver had built a dam on Cherry Creek meant to

The 1965 Denver flood destroyed homes, businesses, and bridges and caused $508 million in damage. As a result, dams were built.

contain floodwaters. But that summer, the South Platte and East and West Plum Creek also flooded, becoming one giant, raging river that swept away bridges, cars, and homes. Six people died, and $508 million in damage was done. After that disaster, the Chatfield and Deer Creek dams were built.

Although flooding sometimes occurs, a bigger problem is water shortages. Colorado's rivers supply water to nineteen U.S. states. The Colorado River alone supplies water and power to twenty-five million people in seven states. When the weather is warmer than usual, the snow melts faster and evaporates, rather than feeding the rivers. This is what made 2002 and 2004 among the ten driest years on record

The Colorado Rockies

Before the Rocky Mountains, there were the Ancestral Rockies, a mountain range that spanned Colorado, Texas, New Mexico, and Colorado. It is a mystery how they formed, but scientists know they existed about 320 to 270 million years ago. Then they eroded.

Millions of years later, during the Jurassic age, parts of California, Idaho, Nevada, and Utah made up a subcontinent apart from North America. When it collided with what was then the West Coast, mountains were created. The pressure reached Colorado forty to seventy million years ago. The land folded up, and the Rocky Mountains were born. This is called the Laramide Oregeny. Even as the mountains rose, they eroded. Rivers and streams raced downhill, scraping sediment off the surface and depositing it in the lowlands.

Twenty-eight to five million years ago, the land between Nevada and central Kansas rose by about 5,000 feet (1,524 m). Lowlands became high plains. Mountains rose higher. Rivers picked up speed. This uplift stretched the land. Cracks released lava, which covered much of the state.

Next, two million years ago, the Pleistocene epoch brought ice ages. Glaciers blanketed the mountains above 8,000 feet (2,438 m), eroding the land. A period of uplift began again.

Today, periodic uplift of the land might still be occurring. Erosion by snow, water, and wind continues. Sediment from earlier erosion is 13,000 feet (3,962 m) deep around Denver, and it extends far beyond the city. The glaciers from the Pleistocene epoch have melted. Tiny glaciers still dot the mountain tops, but they are only about three thousand years old, and they are shrinking.

The Ancestral Rockies produced basins that are rich in oil today. In Colorado and New Mexico, the Rocky Mountains now overlay the evidence of the Ancestral Rockies.

in Colorado. Meanwhile, in the 1990s, Colorado's population grew by 30 percent. Water use grew in other states, too. Even with conservation efforts and new technologies, the Colorado River hasn't been able to keep up with demand.

The state's many rivers, forests, mountains, and plains are home to a wide range of animals, including bears, mountain lions, mountain goats, moose, elk, deer, minks, and several species of mice and rats. The state animal is

Bighorn sheep are some of the many wild animals living in the Rocky Mountains. Others include bears, mountain lions, wolves, minks, moose, and elk.

the bighorn sheep. Fish include the razorback sucker, the cutthroat trout, and the pike minnow—at around 80 pounds (36 kilograms), the largest minnow in North America. Birds include the mountain bluebird, the lark bunting (the state bird), and the peregrine falcon, considered the fastest creature on Earth. (It swoops down at 200 miles [322 km] per hour to catch prey.) Unfortunately, many of Colorado's creatures, such as the gray wolf, black-footed ferret, boreal toad, and grizzly bear, are endangered.

As cities grow, animal habitats shrink. To minimize their impact, people are learning to coexist with the animals. It is illegal to feed deer, elk, mountain goats, and other animals, as this causes the population to grow too fast. People are asked not to let pets roam, as they

11

could injure young wildlife. In mountain towns, residents lock up their trash to deter bears. Signs also alert people when bears, mountain lions, or coyotes have been seen. That means it's not safe for kids and pets to play outside alone.

The plants of Colorado are as diverse as the climate and terrain. Forests are home to pines, firs, and aspens. The plains and plateau are known for their short grasses and sagebrush. High in the mountains, tundra plants and flowers grow near the ground to conserve energy and protect themselves from the wind. Throughout Colorado, meadows are filled with beautiful wildflowers, including the columbine, the state flower.

Chapter 2

THE HISTORY OF COLORADO

The first people in Colorado were the Paleo-Indians, who arrived about twelve thousand years ago. They hunted the big-game animals of the ice age. As the climate warmed, plants and animals changed. Around seven thousand years ago, people began hunting smaller game and gathering wild plants in the Archaic period. As tribes began to make ceramic bowls, hunt with bows and arrows, and, in some cases, farm, they entered the Ceramic period. This began about two thousand years ago.

Perhaps the best known tribe of the Ceramic period are the Anasazi, ancestors of today's Pueblos. Living in southwestern Colorado, Utah, Arizona, and New Mexico, they engineered pueblos with as many as eight hundred rooms that housed thousands of people. In the thirteenth century, they relocated to equally elaborate cliff dwellings high up in canyon walls. After a short time, they mysteriously moved south, to Arizona and New Mexico. Nobody knows why. Archaeologists think drought played a role. But they also think there was a second factor—either a civil war over land and water, threats from an enemy tribe, or a change in religious beliefs.

The Utes became the major tribe in western Colorado. East of the Rockies, the Apache, Comanche, Cheyenne, Arapaho, Kiowa, and

The Anasazi lived in cliff dwellings like these in Mesa Verde National Park. During the thirteenth century, the inhabitants mysteriously moved to what is now Arizona and New Mexico. They are ancestors of the Pueblo people.

Navajo lived. The arrival of Europeans in the 1500s would ultimately lead to the removal of tribes from Colorado.

The Spanish were the first European explorers in Colorado. They were joined by the French in the 1600s. Many tribes dealt peacefully with the newcomers, but the Comanches resisted them, raiding settlement camps.

In 1803, the French sold Colorado lands to the United States as part of the Louisiana Purchase. Now the region needed to be explored and mapped. In 1806, Lieutenant Zebulon Pike explored Colorado. Pikes Peak is named for him, though he didn't climb it.

By then, trappers had come to Colorado in search of beavers. The supply dwindled in a matter of decades. However, some trappers—called mountain men—stayed in Colorado, guiding new-comers through the difficult mountain terrain.

Rich farmland drew others to the area. San Luis in southern Colorado was settled by Spanish settlers in 1851. They farmed the land and grazed animals in common pastureland, which still exists today. San Luis is the oldest living town in Colorado.

That same year, several tribes signed a peace treaty with the settlers. The Utes and Jicarilla Apaches resisted until 1855, when they, too, agreed to treaties. It was an uneasy peace, however. As settlers flooded Colorado in search of gold, they encroached on Native lands, leading to violent battles.

Pikes Peak or Bust

When a small amount of gold was discovered near present-day Denver in 1858, men from the nearby Kansas Territory established a settlement. Denver City was named for James Denver, who had been the Kansas Territory's governor. The next year, the "Pikes Peak or Bust" gold rush was the biggest in history. One hundred thousand people traveled to Colorado. Many returned home empty-handed. Others struck gold in Idaho Springs, Central City, and other mountain towns. Denver grew as a supply center to the mining towns.

Meanwhile, some Native tribes battled newcomers and attacked wagon trains. Massacres by both Native Americans and European Americans occurred. Eventually, the Plains Indians were displaced.

Mined metals needed to be processed. When Nathaniel Hill developed a smelting process and brought it to Denver, the city became the smelting capital of the Rocky Mountains. In 1870, a new railroad provided transportation for mining products. In 1876, Colorado became a state. Because this was one hundred years after

Denver

In 1859, Denver City consisted of one hundred cabins. Nearby Auraria had 250. The following year, the two communities, along with Highland, merged to form Denver. The city supplied nearby mining towns. It also processed and transported the metals. As the population grew from five thousand in 1870 to thirty-five thousand in 1880, lawlessness arose. Saloons and gambling halls opened, which was typical for western cities at the time.

By 1890, Denver had grown to 107,000 people, making it the second biggest city in the west. But it was still a rustic town. In 1904, Mayor Robert Speer vowed to make it a "city beautiful." He planted thousands of trees, landscaped the streets, and spurred a period of new construction. Mining declined in the early 1900s, but Denver no longer relied on the industry to stay afloat. It was large enough to withstand even the worst economic downturns.

Today, Denver has more than two million residents. It is home to professional baseball (the Colorado Rockies), football (the Denver Broncos), basketball (the Denver Nuggets), and hockey (the Colorado Avalanche) teams. With three hundred sunny days a year and nearby mountains, the city attracts people who enjoy the outdoors.

Unfortunately, the growing population has led to sprawl. With no geographical boundaries to rein it in, the city expanded into the foothills. Wild lands became suburbs. Native critters lost their habitats—or had to share them with people.

However, the city is committed to environmentalism. Many people ride their bikes to work, and in 2004, voters passed the FasTracks Initiative, which will bring light rail to the city and suburbs, cutting down on pollution and oil use. The city is also committed to infill—redeveloping areas of downtown and midtown. Today, Denver is illustrating how cities can slow sprawl—and make the sprawl that already exists greener.

America gained independence, Colorado is often called the Centennial State.

The next wave of mining began in 1878 with the Leadville silver boom, which produced millionaires overnight. Soon, silver surpassed gold in mining activity. As Leadville became crowded, prospectors established new camps. They traveled to the San Juan Mountains, which was Ute land. The Utes were the last tribe to be pushed off their Colorado homelands.

The town of Leadville, Colorado, exploded with the 1878 silver boom. Sitting in a scenic mountain valley, it is now a popular tourist destination.

In 1891, the Cripple Creek gold rush produced more overnight millionaires. Two years later, silver mines were dealt a heavy blow. The federal government had promised to purchase 4.5 million ounces of silver per month. Now, Congress repealed the act. Laid-off miners flooded other towns in search of work. Banks closed. Crop prices dropped. Gold became king again. In 1900, Cripple Creek yielded $20 million in gold, making it the second richest mine in the world.

Meanwhile, miners across the state fought for better wages. After a violent conflict between the National Guard and coal miners in 1914, the government ordered coal mine owners to increase wages, decrease work hours, and improve safety conditions. But just as workers were making headway, mining declined in the state.

Mines, including the Cripple Creek gold mine and several gas, coal, rock, and uranium mines, still operate, but not like in the

Before the gold rush, vast and rich farmland drew settlers to Colorado. Now, the San Luis Valley is one of the only places in North America where quinoa, a grain native to Peru, can be grown.

heyday of the 1800s. Some old mining towns, such as Telluride and Georgetown, are now tourist destinations. Others are ghost towns. You can visit Animas Forks, a town at an elevation of 11,584 feet (3,531 m), for a glimpse of life in a mining town. Here, miners who stayed through the winter endured 20 feet (6 m) of snow and the constant threat of avalanches.

As mining declined, agriculture grew. It remains a big business today, especially in the Eastern Plains and Western Plateau. Colorado's population expanded. New industries flourished. Today, Colorado is the third fastest growing state in America.

Chapter 3

THE GOVERNMENT OF COLORADO

As in all states, three branches make up the Colorado government. The legislative branch makes the laws. The judicial branch interprets the laws. The executive branch enforces the laws.

The legislative branch, also known as the general assembly, is divided into two groups: the senate and the house of representatives. In Colorado, the senators and representatives are citizen legislators. When they're not in session, they have jobs in fields such as ranching, teaching, or law.

Colorado has thirty-five state senators, elected every four years. There are sixty-five representatives, elected every two years. The senate elects a president, and the house of representatives elects a speaker of the house.

In the 1920s, the Colorado state government was marred by the Ku Klux Klan. In that decade, thiry-five thousand Coloradoans joined the Klan, and the terrorist group affected the outcome of elections. That has changed. In 2009, both the house and the senate elected their first African American leaders, senate president Peter Groff and Speaker of the House Terrance Carroll.

The Democrats and Republicans each have a caucus, which meets to discuss issues and decide how to vote. Each caucus elects

In 2009, the Colorado house and senate elected their first African American leaders. Terrance Carroll (*left*) is speaker of the house, and Peter Groff (*right*) is senate president.

a majority or minority leader. If there are more Republicans and fewer Democrats, the Republican is the majority leader and the Democrat the minority leader, and vice versa.

Colorado is a swing state. Sometimes its state legislature is majority Republican and other times, majority Democrat. In 2000 and 2004, voters elected President George W. Bush, and in 2008, President Barack Obama. For the most part, Colorado ranchers, farmers, and military families vote Republican, whereas people in cities such as Denver and Boulder vote Democratic.

Both senators and representatives can write and propose bills. Next, bills go to a committee within the house or the senate. Representatives and senators spend most of their time in these meetings. Citizens can also attend and testify or give their opinions. If the committee approves a bill, it is voted on by the house and senate (first by whichever introduced it). If more than half of the house and senate vote in favor, it is approved. Next, the governor can either sign the bill into law or veto it. The Colorado governor has powerful veto power. If he or she vetoes a bill, the legislature needs two-thirds of the senate and house to vote to override the veto. An alternative is to revise the bill and try again with the governor.

Judicial and Executive Branches

The judicial branch interprets state laws and decides whether a person has broken a law. In Colorado, the trial courts include the district courts, county courts, and water courts.

The water courts handle water rights and usage. They decide who can use water from the state's river systems. Most states do not have water courts. Colorado does because many rivers originate in the state, much of that water leaves the state, and water is often in short supply. Seven major river basins in Colorado—the South Platte, the Arkansas, the Rio Grande, the Gunnison, the Colorado, the White, and the San Juan—have a court. Every court has a judge, a clerk, a water referee, and a water engineer. The water referee hears cases first. He or she determines whether one person's water rights would interfere with another person's water rights. If the case isn't settled, it goes before the water judge.

The county courts handle civil matters under $15,000, misdemeanors, traffic incidents, small claims, protection orders, and felony complaints. Felony complaints are often sent to district court, which is a higher court. County court cases can be appealed to the district court. There are 114 county judges, plus 17 Denver County Court judges, who are appointed by the mayor.

There are 22 district courts, with 168 judges, which handle criminal, juvenile, probate, mental health, and civil matters. If a plaintiff or defendant is unhappy with the outcome of a case, he or she can ask the Colorado Court of Appeals to rehear the case. Twenty-two judges make up the court of appeals. Three judges make up a panel that hears a case. Court of appeals decisions can be appealed to the Colorado Supreme Court, the highest court in the state. Its seven

Colorado Law and Order

During the gold and silver booms of the late 1800s, thousands of newcomers flooded Colorado. The population growth of mining towns outpaced the establishment of law and order. There were police, but they couldn't always control the citizens. This led to vigilantism. Citizens went after someone accused of a crime and, without a trial, killed that person. This lead to innocent people being killed by a mob, particularly if the group didn't like the person's nationality or ethnicity.

The silver mining town of Leadville was known for its wild streets filled with saloons and gambling halls. Holdups were commonplace. After the city marshal was murdered by his own deputy in 1879, citizens took matters into their own hands. They lynched an alleged thief and another alleged criminal. To stop the chaos, the mayor and city council organized a volunteer police force to help the paid police. They encouraged church groups and business leaders to establish hospitals and other institutions that would stabilize the town.

Eventually, Leadville grew into a distinguished city, although it suffered when mining declined. It is just one example of how leaders worked to turn Wild West towns into more livable cities.

Now, there is a stable system of police departments and courts in Colorado. Crime still exists, of course, but it is prosecuted in a court of law, not by vigilantes. Today, vigilantes would be prosecuted for the crimes they commit.

In 1893, the price of silver dropped, and Leadville's economy suffered. Millionaires lost their fortunes. The population dwindled from 40,000 to 14,477. To attract tourists and jump-start their economy, business leaders built an Ice Palace, a castle made of 5,000 tons (5,080 tonnes) of ice. It housed a skating rink and ballroom. Though it attracted 250,000 visitors, the Ice Palace lost money.

Soon, Leadville would find a new metal to mine: molybdenum. In the 1980s, that industry, too, collapsed. Facing high unemployment, the town again turned to tourism to rebuild its economy. This time, it worked. People now visit Leadville for its Victorian architecture, mountain beauty, and storied history.

justices make the final decision on state cases that they agree to hear. If the plaintiff or defendant believes the outcome of the case is contrary to the U.S. Constitution, he or she can appeal the case to the U.S. Supreme Court.

The executive branch of the state government carries out the laws of the state and makes sure state affairs run smoothly. In Colorado, the executive branch has five elected officials: the governor, the lieutenant governor, the attorney general, the

The Colorado State Capitol building in Denver is known for its gold-leaf dome. It was completed in 1908, soon after Mayor Robert Speer began his "City Beautiful" campaign.

treasurer, and the secretary of state. The governor heads several offices, including Homeland Security and the Energy Office. He or she also appoints executives to lead several departments, including the departments of education, agriculture, and natural resources. Often, the governor's spouse is a public figure and takes up a cause. A First Lady may advocate for mental health awareness, for instance.

Each executive officer oversees certain boards. For instance, the lieutenant governor oversees Head Start, among other things. He or she also takes the governor's place when needed. The attorney general oversees criminal justice, consumer protection, and other legal matters. The treasurer is charged with state accounting and investing, and unclaimed property. The secretary of state handles administration, licensing, and elections.

Chapter 4

THE ECONOMY OF COLORADO

Silver and gold originally drew settlers to Colorado. While mining has declined, natural resources continue to drive the state economy. Oil is one of the most sought-after resources in Colorado. It brings in more than $20 billion to the state economy annually, and the industry employs more than seventy thousand people.

Agriculture, supported by the fertile Eastern Plains and Western Plateau, is a big business, too. Cattle and sheep ranches and farms growing wheat, corn, hay, and sugar beets create a $5 billion industry. On a smaller scale, Cortez is the pinto bean capital of the world. The region's glacial soil has made it ideal for growing beans, a tradition thousands of years old.

Colorado's best known natural resource, however, is probably its beauty. The dramatic landscape, the snow, and the sun have long drawn people to Colorado. This was especially true after World War II. Colorado's number of tourists grew, as did the economy. In 1940, Winter Park opened to skiers. The 1950s brought Aspen fame as an upscale ski town—and a second home to the rich and famous. Ski resorts in Vail and Purgatory were constructed in the 1960s. Soon, Colorado became known as Ski Country U.S.A.

Summer tourism grew, too. Hikers, campers, and families seeking cooler temperatures headed to the national forests and Rocky

Agriculture in Colorado is a $5 billion industry. Wheat, corn, hay, and sugar beets are top crops. Cattle and sheep ranches are also prevalent.

Mountain National Park. Surrounding towns such as Estes Park and Grand Lake offered tourist mainstays like miniature golf, boating, and shopping. White-water rafting on Colorado's many rivers became a popular activity.

Road improvements made driving to vacation spots easier. Originally, Interstate 70 was going to end in Denver. But beginning in 1956, engineers and workers began the difficult task of building a road through the mountains. In 1961, the Idaho Springs Bypass, just outside of Denver, was created. From 1968 to 1973, workers blasted through the base of the Continental Divide to complete the Eisenhower Tunnel. This gave travelers a straight shot from Denver

Glenwood Springs

In Glenwood Springs, 2,700 gallons of hot spring water rise to the surface every minute. Geologists believe that ground water and trapped volcanic heat may cause the hot springs.

When Ute Indians discovered the hot springs of what is now Glenwood Springs, they named them *Yampah*, meaning "Big Medicine." They soaked in the warm mineral waters to heal and improve their general health. They also sought relaxation and healing in the nearby vapor caves.

In the late 1800s, silver miners pushed the Utes off their land in western Colorado. Walter Devereux bought the hot springs land in 1886 to develop as a vacation destination. Two years later, he and his brothers opened a 615-foot by 75-foot (187 m x 23 m) hot springs pool. A lodge and bathhouse were completed in 1890. The Spa, as it was called, became a popular resort for the rich and famous. Annie Oakley, Doc Holliday, and Al Capone were among the visitors. Doc Holliday sought healing in the hot springs, but died of tuberculosis soon after arriving.

Years later, twenty-two local businessmen bought the lodge and hot springs pool. Now called Glenwood Hot Springs, it is open to the public year-round—even on Christmas. No matter how cold the air is, the hot springs are about 90 to 104 degrees Fahrenheit (32 to 40 degrees Celcius). Heated deep within the earth, the water would naturally be 122°F (50°C). Cool water is added to it. Today, the hot springs have a kiddie pool, water slides, and miniature golf. The lodge is still open for visitors.

The vapor caves are now the Yampah Spa & Salon, a steam room–type cave in which temperatures average 110 to 112°F (43 to 44°C). The hot springs running through the cave (with temperatures climbing to 125°F [52°C]) create the steam. The Yampah caves are the only natural vapor caves in North America.

In 2010, the town turned 125 years old.

to Vail and Aspen—an alternative to following a steep and winding road over the divide. It was one of many tunnels built to improve the state's highways.

Tourism generated new commercial, residential, and road construction, and it supported the economies of mountain towns. While it was good for the economy, Coloradoans worried that tourism was harming the state's natural beauty. When given the opportunity to

Tourists spend $8 billion annually in Colorado on activities such as white-water rafting. They are attracted by the beauty, the outdoor activities, and the climate.

host the 1976 Winter Olympics, the state declined. Residents didn't want the growth and development that would come with it.

However, tourism continues to drive growth in Colorado. Tourists spend $8 billion annually in the state. In addition to Aspen, Telluride has become a popular vacation place for celebrities, including Oprah Winfrey and Tom Cruise.

The western slope enjoyed the latest boom in vacation homes. But the recession of 2008 slowed construction, and many workers in the area lost their jobs.

The beauty of Colorado not only drew tourists after World War II, but many new residents, too. Many residents now spend their weekends on the slopes. As an employee benefit, some companies offer ski passes.

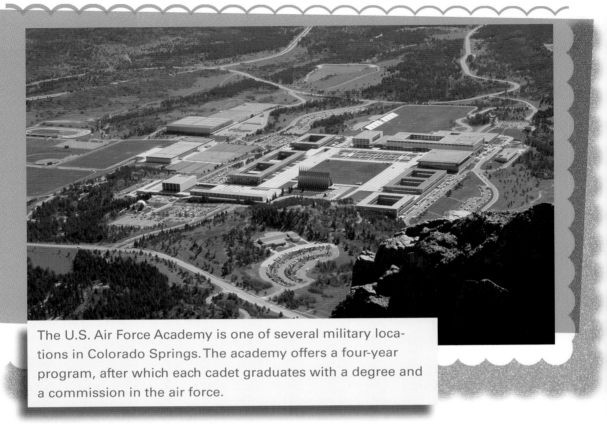

The U.S. Air Force Academy is one of several military locations in Colorado Springs. The academy offers a four-year program, after which each cadet graduates with a degree and a commission in the air force.

Military, High Tech, and Other Industries

Natural resources aren't the only driving force in Colorado's economy. After World War II, the U.S. military became a major employer in Colorado. In the 1940s, several military bases opened, including what is now Peterson Air Force Base in Colorado Springs. It is the third largest employer in the state. In addition, Colorado Springs is home to Schriever Air Force Base, the U.S. Air Force Academy, Cheyenne Mountain Air Force Station, and Fort Carson Army Post.

Weapon and military support companies are also major employers. Mined uranium (used for weapon building) totaled $133 million in Colorado from 1948 to 1960. And in 1953, a nuclear weapon component plant was built in Rocky Flats. Lockheed Martin Space Systems, a global security company, is one of the state's largest employers. In all, the Department of Defense spends $5 billion in the state every year.

Denver is home to a wide range of employers, three of the largest being Alpine Access, a business services company; University of Colorado School of Medicine, a hospital and school; and IBM, a business and IT services company. When Denver International Airport opened in 1995, it became one of the state's biggest employers, as well. In the 1990s, many high-tech businesses opened in Denver. Several folded when the Internet bubble burst in 2000. (Internet-based companies had grown too fast for the economy to support them, and many closed nationwide.) This hurt Denver's economy, but the city rebounded. Today, Colorado has the third highest number of high-tech workers per capita in the country.

Elsewhere, some of the state's biggest employers are Allstate Insurance in Colorado Springs, Colorado State University in Fort Collins, and the University of Colorado in Boulder.

Companies with their headquarters in Colorado include Chipotle Mexican Grill, Red Robin Gourmet Burgers, Rocky Mountain Chocolate Factory, and Time Warner Telecom, Inc. Several oil and gold companies are headquartered in Colorado, including the Cripple Creek gold mine, still in operation.

Statewide, the leading Colorado industries, according to the Bureau of Labor Statistics, are trade, transportation, and utilities (these three are lumped together), followed by government and then professional and business services. These three, and education and health, are typical leaders in employment in American states. In Colorado, however, leisure and hospitality are the fourth biggest employers, followed by education and health.

Chapter 5

PEOPLE FROM COLORADO:
PAST AND PRESENT

Many figures from history, the entertainment industry, sports, science, business, and literature were born or found success in Colorado.

Historical Figures

John Henry "Doc" Holliday (1851–1887) Doc Holliday is buried in Glenwood Springs, even though he only spent a short time there. Although he practiced dentistry in several western states, Holliday is better known for his gambling and gun slinging, particularly the shoot-out at the O.K. Corral. Suffering from tuberculosis, Holliday traveled to Colorado to soak up the mineral waters of Glenwood Springs. He never recovered, dying three months after coming to the state.

Chief Ouray (1833–1880) Chief Ouray was raised by a Spanish family in New Mexico. As a young man, he joined his father, who had become a Ute chief in Colorado. When he emerged as a major leader of the Ute people, he knew the U.S. Army was too powerful to fight. Instead, he used diplomacy to try to keep the Ute land. Ultimately, the Utes were pushed off most of their land, a fate most historians believe was inevitable, whether it happened violently or peacefully.

Music

Katherine Lee Bates (1859–1929) A writer and college professor, Katherine Lee Bates lectured at Colorado College in 1893. That summer, she hiked to the top of Pikes Peak. After a difficult climb, she was awe-struck by the view. She wrote all four verses of "America the Beautiful" at that moment. It has since become America's unofficial anthem.

Erie Photo Co.,   D. B. Chase.

Chief Ouray, pictured in 1875, knew the U.S. Army was too powerful to fight. As a leader of the Ute people, he used diplomacy to try to keep the Ute land.

John Denver (1943–1997) Born John Henry Deutschdorf in Roswell, New Mexico, Denver changed his name at the age of twenty-one. Hopeful of entering show business, he thought the name "Denver" had a better ring to it. He and his wife, Annie, moved to Aspen in 1970. For the next decade, he wrote many hit songs, including "Rocky Mountain High," which became one of Colorado's state songs. In 1997, Denver

John Denver, pictured in 1975, was born in New Mexico but spent much of his life in Colorado. He changed his last name from Deutschdorf to Denver, after the capital of the state he loved.

was flying a private plane when it ran out of fuel. He died in the crash.

The Fray (2002–) Isaac Slade and Joe King grew up together in the Denver suburbs. When they ran into each other at a Littleton music store, they decided to jam together. They were joined by Slade's schoolmates Dave Welsh and Ben Wysocki and became The Fray. A Boulder station was the first to play the band's "Cable Car (In Over My Head)." The Fray was signed to Epic Records. When the TV show *Grey's Anatomy* used "How to Save a Life" in its ads, it became the best-selling digital album of all time. The band still lives in Denver.

Entertainment

Tim Allen (1953–) Tim Allen was born in Denver. After a rough period in his life, he decided to try stand-up comedy. He performed at the Comedy Castle in Detroit before landing on cable comedy specials. Eventually, he starred in the sitcom *Home Improvement*. He is now best known as the star of *The Santa Clause* movies.

Mary Chase (1907–1981) Born in Denver, Mary Chase went to work for the *Rocky Mountain News* at age eighteen. She was promoted to columnist but quit the paper in the 1930s to raise her children and be a freelance writer. She wrote several plays that became Broadway shows or movies, including *Harvey*, which won the Pulitzer Prize for drama in 1945 and is slated for a remake by Steven Spielberg.

Life for the Ute Tribe

Before the Europeans came to America, several bands of Utes lived in New Mexico, Arizona, Utah, and Colorado. In spring and summer, small groups hunted and gathered plants in the mountains. In late fall, these groups gathered in the valleys. They shared food, did the traditional Bear Dance, and arranged marriages.

In the late 1500s, the Spanish arrived in western America. The Utes traded with them, especially for horses, which allowed them to hunt farther away. The Ute way of life changed, but they retained their land.

During the gold and silver rush three hundred years later, American settlers arrived from the East. The newcomers depleted the wildlife and polluted the streams. They wanted the Utes pushed out. Some Utes fought. Others negotiated peace treaties. The U.S. government didn't honor the treaties, and eventually the Utes were forced to give up most of their land.

Many Utes left Colorado for a reservation in Utah. Those who stayed moved onto two adjoining reservations in southwest Colorado: the Southern Ute Reservation and the Ute Mountain Ute Reservation.

Today, the Ute Mountain Ute Reservation has a casino, construction enterprise, farming enterprise, and grazing lands. Nearly two thousand people live on the reservation, and it employs nine hundred people.

The Southern Ute Reservation has a motel, casino, cultural center, gas and oil company, and large park where people hunt, fish, and ride horses. Agriculture has replaced the Ute's nomadic lifestyle, but they retain many cultural traditions, including the ancient Bear Dance.

Sports

Jack Dempsey (1895–1983) Born in Manassa, Colorado, in 1895, William Harrison "Jack" Dempsey boxed in mining towns as a teenager under the name Kid Blackie. By age twenty-four, he had won eighty professional matches. In a brutal 1919 match, he beat the much bigger Jess Willard to become heavyweight champion. After losing the title to Gene Tunney, he opened a restaurant in New York.

John Elway (1960–) A college football and baseball star, John Elway was recruited by the New York Yankees and drafted by the Baltimore Colts in 1983. He chose football but refused to sign with the Colts. Instead, he spent his entire career with the Denver Broncos. He led the team to five Super Bowls and won two rings in 1998 and 1999.

Dr. Edwin James (1797–1861) Pikes Peak is named for Zebulon Montgomery Pike, the first settler to try to climb the mountain. Due to a blizzard, he never made it to the top. Dr. Edwin James and two other explorers reached the peak in 1820. The explorers named the mountain after James, but everybody called it Pikes Peak, which became its official name.

Science

Scott Carpenter (1925–) A Boulder native, Scott Carpenter was both an astronaut and an aquanaut. As an astronaut, he flew the *Aurora 7* around Earth. As an aquanaut, he lived in a sea lab on the ocean floor for thirty days as part of the Navy's Man-at-Sea program. He now lives in Vail with his family.

Robert Seiwald (1925–) Fort Morgan native Robert Seiwald, along with Joseph Burckhalter, invented FITC, a compound used for identifying antigens. Antigens are bacteria or viruses that cause diseases. FITC is used in diagnosing AIDS and leukemia. Seiwald is in the National Inventors Hall of Fame.

Business

Ruth Handler (1916–2002) Born in Denver, Ruth Handler started a plastic furniture company with her husband, Elliot. Under the company name Mattel, they began making toy furniture and other toys. While visiting Europe with their teenagers, Barbara and Ken, the Handlers saw a doll that wasn't a baby but an adult woman. Mattel created its own adult doll, Barbie, which debuted in 1959.

W. S. Stratton (1848–1902) Winfield Scott Stratton was a carpenter in Colorado Springs. His side job was prospecting for gold. In 1891, he found it and became Cripple Creek's first millionaire. He stayed in the humble home that he had built and gave much of his money away. He donated land for the city hall, post office, and other Colorado Springs buildings. When he died, he willed his money to a home for homeless children and elderly people.

Denver native Ruth Handler founded Mattel with her husband. The company created the Barbie doll after the Handler family, while visiting Europe, saw an adult doll there.

George Turner In 1915, George Turner, a moving company owner, began building old-fashioned, child-sized buildings for his daughter. He opened the pint-sized village to the public in 1920, calling it Tiny Town. Through the years, it fell into disrepair, but today it operates as a successful not-for-profit park.

Timeline

12,000 years ago	The Paleo-Indians first arrive in Colorado.
Late 1300s	The Anasazi leave their cliff dwellings and head south. The Utes populate western Colorado.
1500s–1600s	The Spanish explore Colorado.
1800	The Spanish cede the land west of the Mississippi to the French.
1803	The French sell the land to the United States as part of the Louisiana Purchase.
1820	Dr. Edwin James is the first known person to scale Pikes Peak.
1851	Several tribes sign a peace treaty with the U.S. government.
1858	Placer gold is found near Denver, beginning the gold rush.
1861	Colorado becomes a territory.
1876	Colorado becomes a state.
1878	The Leadville silver boom begins. As prospectors move into the San Juan Mountains, the Utes are displaced.
1889	Phone lines are laid along Mosquito Pass.
Early 1900s	Miners fight for better wages and safer work conditions. They gain ground, but the mining industry declines.
1940s	Several military bases open in Colorado. Winter Park opens as a ski resort.
1950s	Aspen becomes an upscale ski town.
1973	The Eisenhower Tunnel is completed.
1990s	The tech boom brings economic growth to Denver. The Internet bubble bursts, hurting the economy. It rebounds, and Denver remains one of the top employers of high-tech workers.
1995	Denver Airport is completed.
2004	Denver voters pass the FasTracks Initiative, bringing light rail to the city.
2008	Colorado hosts the Democratic National Convention.

State motto:	*Nil sine Numine* ("Nothing Without the Deity")
State capital:	Denver
State tree:	Colorado blue spruce
State flower:	White and lavender columbine
State bird:	Lark bunting
Year of statehood:	1876 (thirty-eighth state)
State nickname:	The Centennial State
Total area and U.S. rank:	104,100 square miles (269,617 sq km); eighth largest state
Population:	4,301,000
Highest elevation:	Mount Elbert, at 14,431 feet (4,399 m)
Lowest elevation:	Arkansas River near the town of Holly, at 3,315 feet (1,010 m)

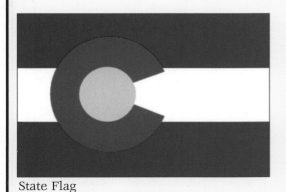

State Flag

State Seal

Major rivers:	Colorado River, North Platte River, South Platte River, Arkansas River, Republican River, Rio Grande, Gunnison River, White River, San Juan River
Major lakes:	Blue Mesa Reservoir, Grand Lake, Lake San Cristobal
Hottest recorded temperature:	118 degrees Fahrenheit (47.7 degrees C), July 11, 1888, in Bennett
Coldest recorded temperature:	61 degrees Fahrenheit (-51.6 degrees Celcius), February 1, 1985, in Maybell
Origin of state name:	"Colorado" means "colored red" in Spanish. The Spanish named the state for its red rocks.
Chief agricultural products:	Cattle, sheep, hay, wheat, corn, sugar beets
Major industries:	Oil, tourism, trade/transportation/utilities, business services, government/military

Lark bunting

Columbine

Anasazi A people who lived in western Colorado until the thirteenth century. They are the ancestors of the Pueblos. The name, given by Navajos, means "foreigner" or "enemy."

centennial The one hundredth year; in America, it refers to 1876, the one hundredth anniversary of gaining independence.

Colorado Plateau The area of elevated land west of the Colorado Rockies.

erosion The breaking down of land by wind, water, or ice.

executive branch The branch of the government that enforces the law.

Great Plains The valleys and plains of North America running from Canada to Texas, and west to the Colorado Rockies.

ice age Any time period in which much of Earth's surface was covered with glaciers; during the last ice age, much of the Rockies were capped with ice.

irrigate To engineer natural water sources to provide water to farmlands.

judicial branch The branch of the government that interprets the law.

legislative branch The branch of the government that makes the law.

Louisiana Purchase Land running from Canada to Louisiana, and from the Rocky Mountains to the Mississippi, which France sold to the United States for $15 million.

mountain men Frontiersmen who lived in the wilderness, either trapping or guiding new settlers over the difficult terrain.

placer gold Gold that is contained in eroded sediment, such as sand, gravel, or water.

Rocky Mountains The mountain range running from Alaska to New Mexico.

uplift Any process that results in a large land area rising to a higher elevation.

Ute One of many Native American tribes that first lived in Colorado. Its people are the last to live as a tribe in the state.

Colorado Historical Society

1300 Broadway

Denver, CO 80203

(303) 866-3682

Web site: http://www.coloradohistory.org

The Colorado Historical Society archives and presents information about the state's past.

Colorado State University

Office of Admissions

1062 Campus Delivery

Fort Collins, CO 80523-1062

(970) 491-6909

Web site: http://www.colostate.edu

Located in Fort Collins, Colorado State University is one of the state's biggest universities.

Environment Colorado

1536 Wynkoop Street, First Floor, Suite 100

Denver, CO 80202

(303) 573-3871

Web site: http://www.environmentcolorado.org/about-us

Environment Colorado is a citizen's group that advocates for the environment.

Manitou Cliff Dwellings

P.O. Box 272

Manitou Springs, CO 80829

(800) 354-9971

Web site: http://www.cliffdwellingsmuseum.com

The museum allows people to explore real Anasazi cliff dwellings and learn about the ancient Pueblo tribe's history.

Southern Ute Museum and Cultural Center

14826 Highway 172

Ignacio, CO 81137

(970) 563-4649

Web site: http://www.southernutemuseum.org

Located on the Southern Ute Reservation, the museum and cultural center archives and presents information about the tribe's history.

University of Colorado Boulder

Office of Admissions

Regent Administrative Center

125 University of Colorado at Boulder

552 UCB

Boulder, CO 80309-0552

(303) 492-6301

Web site: http://www.colorado.edu

The University of Colorado Boulder is one of Colorado's biggest schools.

Western Museum of Mining & Industry

225 North Gate Boulevard

Colorado Springs, CO 80921

(800) 752-6558

Web site: http://www.wmmi.org

The museum educates people about mining in the past and present.

Web Sites

Due to the changing nature of Internet links, Rosen Publishing has developed an online list of Web sites related to the subject of this book. This site is updated regularly. Please use this link to access the list:

http://www.rosenlinks.com/uspp/copp

FOR FURTHER READING

Bograd, Larry. *Uniquely Colorado* (Heinemann State Studies). Portsmouth, NH: Heinemann, 2003.

Chase, Mary. *Harvey*. New York, NY: Dramatists Play Service, 1999.

Gardiner, Lisa. *Catastrophic Colorado: The History and Science of Our Natural Disasters*. Boulder, CO: Westcliffe Publishers, 2006.

Gerber, Robin. *Barbie and Ruth: The Story of the World's Most Famous Doll and the Woman Who Created Her*. New York, NY: HarperCollins, 2009.

McAuliffe, Bill. *The Colorado Avalanche* (The NHL: History and Heroes). Mankato, MN: Creative Education, 2008.

Omoth, Tyler. *The Story of the Colorado Rockies*. Mankato, MN: Creative Education, 2007.

Oswald, Nancy. *Nothing Here but Stones: A Jewish Pioneer Story*. New York, NY: Henry Holt & Co., 2004.

Ray, Deborah Kogan. *Down the Colorado: John Wesley Powell, the One-Armed Explorer*. New York, NY: Farrar, Straus & Giroux, 2007.

Roberts, Gary L. *Doc Holliday: The Life and Legend*. Hoboken, NJ: Wiley, 2007.

Roberts, Randy. *Jack Dempsey: The Manassa Mauler*. Champaign, IL: University of Illinois Press, 2003.

Rozinski, Bob. *On the Trail of Colorado Critters*. Boulder, CO: Westcliffe Publishers, 2000.

Somervill, Barbara. *Colorado* (America the Beautiful). New York, NY: Scholastic, 2008.

BIBLIOGRAPHY

Abbot, Carl, Stephen Leonard, and Thomas Noel. *Colorado: A History of the Centennial State*. 4th ed. Boulder, CO: University Press of Colorado, 2005.

Chronic, Halka, and Felicie Williams. *Roadside Geology of Colorado*. 2nd ed. Missoula, MT: Mountain Press Publishing, 2002.

City of Colorado Springs. "History of Pikes Peak." Retrieved October 11, 2009 (http://www.springsgov.com/Page.aspx?NavID=86).

Collier, Joseph, and Grant Collier. *Colorado: Yesterday & Today*. Lakewood, CO: Collier Publishing, 2005.

Colorado Division of Local Government. "Population Totals for U.S. and States." State Demography Office. Retrieved October 14, 2009 (http://www.dola.state.co.us/demog/pop_us_estimates.html).

Colorado: The Official Site of Colorado Tourism. "Town of San Luis." 2009. Retrieved October 6, 2009 (http://www.colorado.com/Articles.aspx?aid=42178).

Colorado: The Official State Web Portal. "Home Page." 2009. Retrieved October 8, 2009 (http://www.colorado.gov).

Fox, Zach. "Oil and Gas Lead GDP." *Denver Post*, July 17, 2007. Retrieved October 3, 2009 (http://www.coloradosenatenews.com/content/view/555/35).

Glenwood Guide. "Doc Holliday." Retrieved October 10, 2009 (http://www.glenwoodguide.com/docholiday.htm).

Glenwood Hot Springs. "History of the Glenwood Hot Springs." Retrieved October 6, 2009 (http://www.hotspringspool.com/images/UserFiles/File/12%20history.pdf).

Harvard Square Library. "Poets of Cambridge, U.S.A.: Katherine Lee Bates." 2006. Retrieved October 10, 2009 (http://www.harvardsquarelibrary.org/poets/bates.php).

Hopkins, Ralph Lee. *Hiking Colorado's Geology*. Seattle, WA: The Mountaineers, 2000.

Johnson, George. "Social Strife May Have Exiled Ancient Indians." August 20, 1996. Retrieved October 10, 2009 (http://www.santafe.edu/~johnson/articles.anasazi.html).

Jornayvaz, Auna. "The Fray Take 2." *Denver Magazine*, October 31, 2008. Retrieved October 10, 2009 (http://www.denvermagazine.com/culture/2008/10/fray-take-2).

Metro Denver. "Industries." 2009. Retrieved October 10, 2009 (http://www.metrodenver.org/industries-companies/industries).

Metzger, Stephen. *Colorado* (Moon Handbooks). Berkeley, CA: Perseus Books, 2009.

NASA. "Scott Carpenter: NASA Astronaut." January 2004. Retrieved October 12, 2009 (http://www.jsc.nasa.gov/Bios/htmlbios/carpenter-ms.html).

National Inventors Hall of Fame. "Robert Seiwald." Retrieved October 11, 2009 (http://www.invent.org/hall_of_fame/130.html).

National Park Service. "Dinosaur and Dinosaur National Monument." April 2000. Retrieved October 4, 2009 (http://www.nps.gov/archive/dino/dinos.htm).

Netstate.com. "Colorado: The Geography of Colorado." Retrieved October 14, 2009 (http://www.netstate.com/states/geography/co_geography.htm).

Official Site of Jack Dempsey. "Biography." Retrieved October 8, 2009 (http://www.cmgww.com/sports/dempsey/biography.htm).

Official Web Site of John Elway. "John Elway Bio." 2009. Retrieved October 11, 2009 (http://www.johnelway.com/johnelwaybio.aspx).

PBS.org. "Who Made America?: Ruth Handler." Retrieved October 12, 2009 (http://www.pbs.org/wgbh/theymadeamerica/whomade/handler_hi.html).

Schriever Air Force Base. "Home Page." Retrieved October 3, 2009 (http://www.mybaseguide.com/air-force/schriever-afb).

Southern Ute Museum and Cultural Center. "Colorado Ute Legacy." Retrieved October 16, 2009 (http://www.southernutemuseum.org/index.cfm?fa = page.display& page_id = 47).

Spellman, Jim. "Colorado Political Leaders Make American History." CNN.com, January 7, 2009. Retrieved October 8, 2009 (http://www.cnn.com/2009/POLITICS/01/07/colorado.legislature/index.html).

Stockman, Tom. "W. S. Stratton: Benefactor of Colorado Springs." *Colorado Adventure Guide: Heritage and History*. Retrieved October 11, 2009 (http://www.coloradovacation.com/history/colorado-springs-william-stratton.html).

StormCenter Communications. "Our Colorado Headwaters." Retrieved October 2, 2009 (http://kmgh.envirocast.net/?pagename = OurWatershed).

Svaldi, Aldo. "Colorado Rural Counties Taking a Beating in Economy." *Denver Post*, September 27, 2009. Retrieved October 10, 2009 (http://www.denverpost.com/search/ci_13425122).

Tiny Town. "Home Page." Retrieved October 9, 2009 (http://www.tinytownrailroad.com).

Ute Mountain Ute. "Overview and Statistics." Retrieved October 20, 2009 (http://www.utemountainute.com/overview_statistics.htm).

Wood, Richard. *Here Lies Colorado: Fascinating Figures in Colorado History*. Helena, MT: Farcountry Press, 2005.

INDEX

About the Author

A former newspaper reporter, Bridget Heos is the author of nine nonfiction books for young adults. She lives in Kansas City with her husband and three sons. With family living in Colorado, she grew up going to Denver and Estes Park every summer.

Photo Credits

Cover (top left) Archive Holdings, Inc./Getty Images; cover (top right) Doug Pensinger/ Getty Images; cover (bottom) © www.istockphoto.com/Erick Todd; pp. 3, 6, 13, 19, 24, 30, 38, 40 (right) Shutterstock.com; p. 4 (top) © GeoAtlas, Inc.; p. 7 © David Muenker/ Alamy; p. 8 Don Grail/Visuals Unlimited/Getty Images; p. 9 Denver Public Library, Western History Collection, X-29252; p. 11 Paul Chesley/National Geographic/Getty Images; p. 14 Philippe Bourseiller/The Image Bank/Getty Images; p. 17 Library of Congress Prints and Photographs Division; p. 18 Jay S. Simon/Stone/Getty Images; p. 20 © AP Images; p. 23 © www.istockphoto.com/Gregory Olsen; p. 25 © www.istock photo.com/Ben Klaus; p. 27 © www.istockphoto.com/Ben Blankenburg; p. 28 U.S. Air Force Academy (http://www.usafa.edu/df/dfan/aero/posting.cfm); p. 31 Transcendental Graphics/Hulton Archives/Getty Images; p. 32 Frank Driggs Collection/Hulton Archive/Getty Images; p. 37 Matt Campbell/AFP/Getty Images; p. 39 (left) Courtesy of Robesus, Inc.; p. 40 (left) © www.istockphoto.com/Bob Balestri.

Designer: Les Kanturek; Editor: Bethany Bryan; Photo Researcher: Cindy Reiman